The Best Book of
Weather

Simon Adams

KINGFISHER

NEW YORK

Contents

Created for Kingfisher Publications
Plc by Picthall & Gunzi Limited

Author: Simon Adams
Consultant: Ron Lobeck
Editor: Lauren Robertson
Designer: Floyd Sayers
Illustrators: Mike Saunders,
  Roger Stewart

KINGFISHER
a Houghton Mifflin Company imprint
215 Park Avenue South
New York, New York 10003
www.houghtonmifflinbooks.com

Published in hardback in 2001
This edition first published in 2002
10 9 8 7 6 5 4 3 2 1

SBF/0602/WKT/MAR(MAR/128KMA

LIBRARY OF CONGRESS CATALOGING-IN-PUBLICATION DATA
has been applied for.

ISBN 0-7534-5584-6

Printed in Hong Kong

4 What is weather?

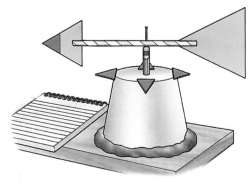

6 Weather and us

14 When the wind blows

16 A world of water

24 Fun in the snow

26 The wildest weather

8 Weather through the ages

10 Climate and seasons

12 The power of the Sun

18 Cloud cover

20 Electric skies

22 All fogged up

28 Spectacular skies

30 Climate in crisis

31 Glossary

32 Index

What is weather?

Earth is wrapped in a thick layer of air called the atmosphere.

This air is made up of gases, and it can be hot or cold, wet or dry, and can move fast or stay still. The changes in the air closest to Earth are known as the weather. The Sun's rays keep our bodies warm. Clouds keep us cool by day and warm at night. Winds blow the clouds around the sky. And rain helps plants grow, and fills our rivers and lakes.

The atmosphere

High above Earth, the atmosphere stretches 500 miles into space. Scientists have divided it into five invisible layers. These layers are made up of a mixture of gases, such as oxygen and nitrogen. We use satellites in the highest layer to take pictures of the weather below. Experts on the ground can then tell us what the weather will be like in the next few days or weeks.

Satellite

Exosphere
This layer lies 435–500 mi. from Earth. It is made up of thin gases that drift off into space. This is where satellites orbit our planet.

Space shuttle

Thermosphere
This layer lies 50–435 mi. from Earth. It is the hottest part of the atmosphere, where aurora lights appear and meteorites burn out.

Aurora lights

Shooting stars

Mesosphere
The mesosphere is 30–50 mi. from Earth and is the coldest part of the atmosphere.

Weather balloon

Stratosphere
This layer is 7–30 mi. above the ground. Airplanes fly in the thin air of the stratosphere.

Airplane

Troposphere
The troposphere is up to 7 mi. above the ground, and this is where all our weather happens.

Clouds

A weather satellite takes photographs of the weather from space.

Cloud formations are easy to see from space.

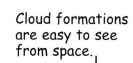

How weather is made

The weather is created by a mixture of water, heat, and air. The Sun heats up the air, which makes it move. This moving air is called wind, and it carries heat and water vapor, which is an invisible gas. Clouds, rain, snow, and fog are made from water vapor.

Walkers stand on a hillside watching the weather change.

Weather and us

The weather affects our daily lives, so scientists try to tell us what it will be like in the days ahead. This is called weather forecasting. The study of the weather is called meteorology, and the scientists who do this are called meteorologists. They use temperature, wind speed, air pressure measurements, and satellite photographs to forecast the weather.

Light helium gas lifts a weather balloon high into the atmosphere so the instruments it carries can record the weather.

Cameras in weather satellites take pictures of weather formations.

Watching the weather

Weather stations on land and at sea, airplanes, weather balloons, and satellites in space are all used for watching and measuring the weather. They help scientists make a weather forecast.

A thermometer measures temperature.

An anemometer records wind speed.

Weather airplanes are used for watching the weather from the sky.

A barometer measures air pressure. Changes in air pressure are recorded by a barograph (below).

Weather maps show weather formations.

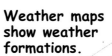

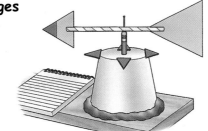

A weather vane shows wind direction.

Weather stations at sea record changes.

Weather power

The weather can be used to make energy that does not cause pollution. Heat from the Sun can drive a car or warm a house. Wind power turns wind turbines to pump water. Without the weather, we could use only oil, coal, and gas for our power, and these fuels may run out.

Solar panels on a house use heat from the Sun to heat water and provide warmth.

Giant wind turbines produce electricity.

Panels on solar-powered cars change sunlight into electricity, which is used to drive the car.

Studying the weather

The speed of the wind, the temperature of the air, and the amount of rainfall can all be measured using simple equipment. You can write down what type of weather happens at the same time each day and see how the weather changes over time.

A science class studying the weather

Weather through the ages

Earth's weather is always changing, and these changes affect all living things. Thousands of years ago, cold periods called ice ages or glacial periods covered the Earth with ice. Warm periods, called interglacials, turned parts of the planet into desert. Today we are living in an interglacial period.

The dinosaurs may have died out because they could not breathe when volcanic dust filled the air.

Weather and extinction

Some types of animals and plants can survive when the weather changes suddenly, but others die out, or become extinct. Scientists believe that the dinosaurs were killed by a sudden change in the weather millions of years ago.

Some think that the dust from an erupting volcano filled the sky and turned the Earth dark and cold. Others believe that the dust was caused by a meteorite hitting Earth.

Woolly rhinoceros

Sometimes scientists travel to the coldest places on Earth to carry out research on the weather.

Meteorologists use special equipment to core the ice for samples.

Discovering the past

Scientists can discover what the weather was like in the past by looking at samples of ice, rock, and earth. Ice buried deep in ice caps and glaciers reveals the weather conditions at the time the ice was created, even if it was formed thousands of years ago.

Ice age world

Ten thousand years ago, Earth was much colder than it is today and looked quite different. Large sheets of ice covered one third of the planet. Mammoths and other animals that lived at that time were covered with thick hair to keep out the cold.

Woolly mammoths

Many areas of land on Earth were covered with ice during the recent ice age.

Reindeer

Climate and seasons

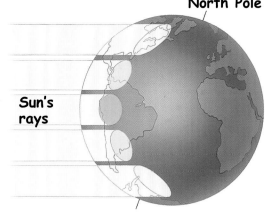

North Pole

Sun's rays

South Pole

The usual weather pattern in a region is called its climate. Different areas of the planet have different climates—places are a combination of mainly hot or cold and wet or dry. The weather changes throughout the year, and these changes are known as the seasons. Most places have four seasons, but some have only two.

Hottest and coldest

The climate is hottest at the equator and coldest at the North and South poles. This is because more of the Sun's rays reach Earth at the equator than at the poles. In the mountains and by the sea, the climate is cooler. Away from the coasts, it is usually hotter and drier by day, but colder at night.

Life at the South Pole is cold and icy.

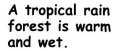

A tropical rain forest is warm and wet.

Many desert areas are hot and dry.

Different climates

The polar climate—at the North and South poles—is very cold. Near the equator, the climate is hot and is described as tropical, or equatorial. In between the poles and the equator are the temperate zones. These are either warm or cool, depending on the time of year.

The changing seasons

Seasons change during the year. When it is winter in the northern part of Earth, or the Northern Hemisphere, it is summer in the southern part, or the Southern Hemisphere.

Spring

Spring is the season when the days grow longer and warmer. Nights are cold, and the weather may change frequently.

Summer

Summer is the hottest season of the year. The Sun is high in the sky, the days are long, and there may be thunderstorms.

Fall

Fall nights get longer, and the days are shorter. The temperature cools down, and leaves may change color and fall off the trees.

Winter

Winter is the coldest season. The Sun is low in the sky, and the days are very short. Snow can fall, icicles form, and rivers and ponds freeze.

Monsoon winds bring heavy rain that floods parts of Asia.

Wet and dry seasons

In East Africa, India, and Southeast Asia there are only two seasons—the wet season and the dry season. In the wet season, the air is humid, and monsoon winds blow in from the sea, carrying heavy rain. In the dry season, monsoon winds blow cool, dry air from the land out to sea.

11

The power of the Sun

Life on Earth would not exist without the Sun's warmth and light. As Earth spins every day on its axis, the side that faces the Sun warms up in the daylight. The side that is hidden from the Sun cools down in the darkness. The change in temperature causes winds to blow, clouds to form, and all other types of weather, such as snow and rain, to develop. It can also lead to floods or droughts.

Too much Sun

People enjoy playing in the Sun and sunbathing in hot weather. But harmful rays from the Sun burn the skin and can cause skin diseases.

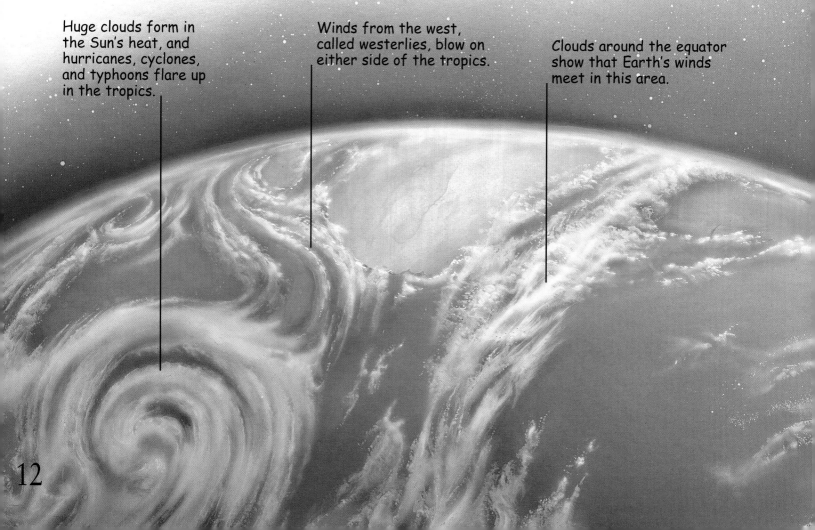

Huge clouds form in the Sun's heat, and hurricanes, cyclones, and typhoons flare up in the tropics.

Winds from the west, called westerlies, blow on either side of the tropics.

Clouds around the equator show that Earth's winds meet in this area.

Sun energy

The Sun affects all our weather. Its heat makes water evaporate, or change into a gas, to form water vapor. The heat also makes the water vapor rise and form clouds. In the tropics the heat of the Sun stirs up moist sea air and creates storm clouds. The Sun also makes the wind blow by heating the air and changing its temperature and pressure.

The Sun's rays travel to Earth 93 million miles away.

Drought

Many hot parts of the planet have long periods with no rain, and this can cause droughts. The heat makes rivers dry up, causing cracks to appear on the land. Crops cannot grow, so people do not have enough food to eat.

The Sun's heat makes water from the ocean evaporate and form clouds.

Earth from space

When the wind blows

Air presses down on us all the time. Cold, heavy air sinks and creates high pressure. This heavy air warms up and keeps the weather fine. Warm air is light, so it rises and creates low pressure. As it rises, new air blows in to take its place. This is called wind. The weather in low pressure conditions is usually wet and windy. Winds can be soft and gentle, or fast and strong.

Measuring the wind

Wind speed is measured in miles per hour using a machine called an anemometer. The Beaufort Scale describes the strength or force of the wind.

1 In forces 0–3, there is no wind or only a light breeze. Clouds drift slowly and the sea is flat or calm.

2 In forces 4–7, the wind is stronger. Trees sway in the breeze and the sea is choppy with waves.

3 In forces 8–12, the wind is fast and powerful. The sea is rough with big waves.

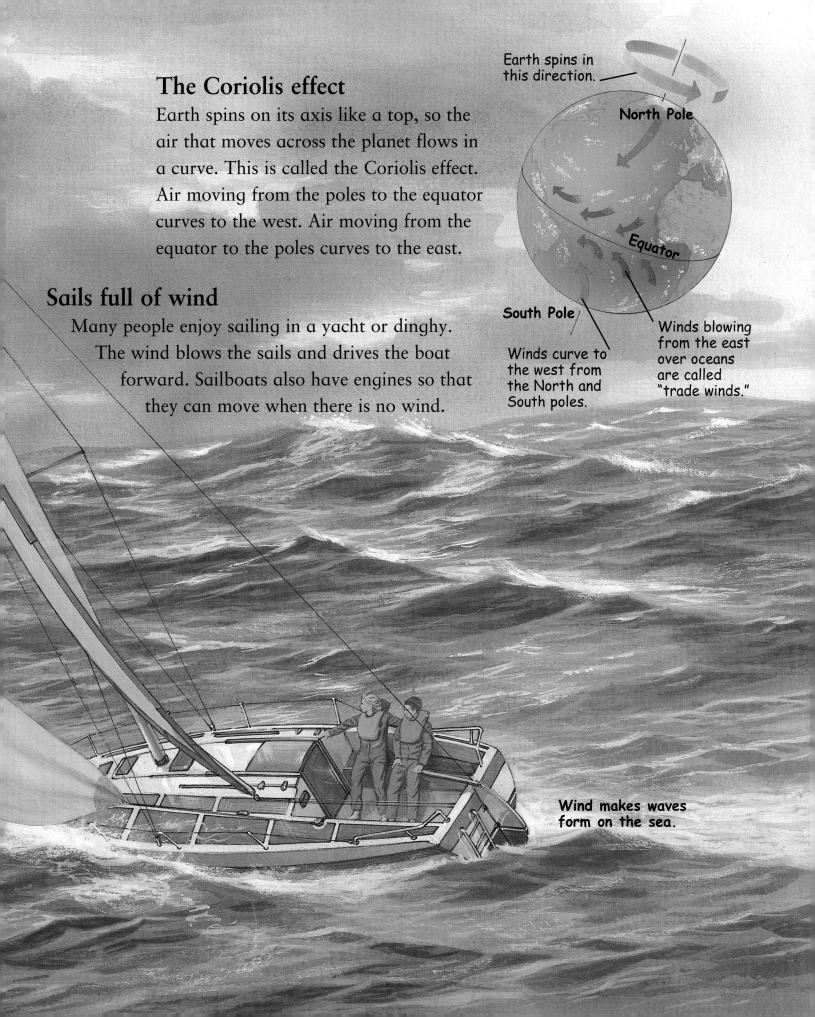

The Coriolis effect

Earth spins on its axis like a top, so the air that moves across the planet flows in a curve. This is called the Coriolis effect. Air moving from the poles to the equator curves to the west. Air moving from the equator to the poles curves to the east.

Sails full of wind

Many people enjoy sailing in a yacht or dinghy. The wind blows the sails and drives the boat forward. Sailboats also have engines so that they can move when there is no wind.

Earth spins in this direction.

North Pole

Equator

South Pole

Winds curve to the west from the North and South poles.

Winds blowing from the east over oceans are called "trade winds."

Wind makes waves form on the sea.

A world of water

The air is full of water vapor that has evaporated from the seas and lakes. As the water vapor cools, it forms droplets of liquid water. These droplets join together and float in the air as clouds. As the water droplets get bigger, they can form huge, dark rain clouds that become so heavy they fall to Earth as raindrops. Clouds disappear after it has rained because all the water in them has fallen to Earth.

The water cycle

Air can soak up and let go of water like a sponge. This means that the water on Earth is always being recycled. The Sun's rays heat seawater, which evaporates to become clouds. These clouds then release raindrops. The rainwater drains back to the sea along streams and rivers to begin the water cycle again.

Vapor cools and forms clouds.

Seawater evaporates in the Sun's heat.

Rainwater flows back to the sea along rivers.

Types of rain

Rain is drops of water falling to the ground from clouds. Small drops are known as drizzle. Larger raindrops fall in showers, and a heavy fall of rain is called a downpour.

Drizzle is small drops of rain falling in a soft spray. There is often drizzle when it is foggy.

A short fall of rain is called a shower. After a shower the sky clears up and the Sun shines again.

A downpour is a heavy fall of rain. The sky is full of dark rain clouds, and puddles form.

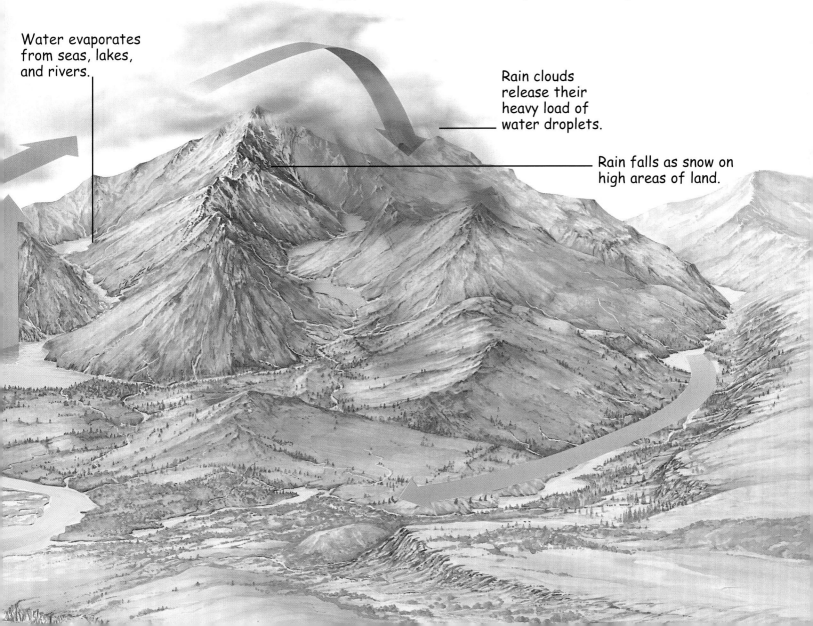

Water evaporates from seas, lakes, and rivers.

Rain clouds release their heavy load of water droplets.

Rain falls as snow on high areas of land.

Cloud cover

Clouds come in many shapes and sizes. Some clouds are layered and look like the scales on a fish. Other clouds look like giant cotton balls in the sky. Some types of clouds can be found close to the ground as fog or mist. Highest in the sky are the cirrus clouds, which are made up of tiny ice crystals. The powerful cumulonimbus clouds are the largest. They tower above all the others, forming an icy wedge on the troposphere.

Cirrus
(6-8 miles above ground)
The highest clouds in the sky are formed from ice crystals where the air is cold. Strong winds blow these clouds into wispy tails. They show that the weather is unsettled.

Altocumulus
(3-4 miles above ground)
These small, fluffy clouds can look like flattened cotton balls that are linked together.

Nimbostratus
(up to half a mile above ground)
These thick, dark layers of rain clouds form close to the ground. They can bring long periods of heavy rain or snow.

Cirrostratus ——————————————————
(6-7 miles above ground)
When sunlight hits ice crystals in
these high-level clouds, a colorful
ring, or halo, can be seen in them.

Cirrocumulus ——————————
(5-6 miles above ground)
Tiny balls of icy cirrocumulus clouds
are known as a "mackerel sky" because
they look like the scales of a fish.

—————— **Altostratus**
(4-5 miles above ground)
These thin, watery layers
of cloud sometimes form
a mist across the sky.

Cumulonimbus ————
(1-6 miles above ground)
Towering cumulonimbus clouds
can bring rain, thunder, and
lightning. These huge thunderclouds
can develop into tornadoes.

Stratocumulus —
(3-4 miles above ground)
The long rolls of cloud made
by cumulus clouds spread out in
layers. They usually mean that
good weather is on the way.

Cumulus
(2-3 miles above ground)
Fluffy, white cumulus clouds do
not last long. As they get bigger
during the day, they can bring rain.

Stratus
(about 1 mile above ground)
These huge, shapeless layers
of clouds are often seen
during periods of rain. ——————

Electric skies

Thunderstorms are often exciting, but they can also be scary. Loud rolls of thunder can be heard many miles away from the heart of the storm. Lightning flashes from the clouds and lights up a dark sky. An electrical charge builds up inside huge, black cumulonimbus clouds. This charge streaks across the sky between clouds as sheet lightning or dramatically strikes the ground as fork lightning, which can damage buildings and trees.

Tree struck by lightning

How distant is a storm?

We can tell how far away a storm is by counting the seconds between the flash of lightning and the clap of thunder. Five seconds equals one mile.

When lightning strikes

Lightning is electrical energy, so it is hot and powerful. Its power lasts only for a few millionths of a second, but it is enough to blow a tree apart.

The power of lightning
Lightning is attracted to metal objects. Buildings are often hit by lightning, so many of them have lightning rods inside them. These metal strips lead the electricity from the lightning safely down to Earth.

All fogged up

Fog is a cloud that forms on the ground. It looks like smoke, but it is actually tiny drops of water that hang in the air. When it is foggy, it is difficult to see things around you, and driving can be dangerous. A thick fog can stop airplanes from taking off and landing. Most forms of transportation have to travel very slowly in fog.

Smog in the city

A thick fog mixed with pollution is called "smog." Most big cities have smog. Pollution and smog can make people sick. Many countries are trying to reduce the amount of smog in their cities by cutting car exhaust fumes and lowering smoke emissions from factories.

In thick fog, boats cannot be seen, so they use lights or foghorns to warn other boats that they are on the water.

A misty morning

Early morning fog on the ground is called mist. It forms after a cool, calm night. When the Sun heats up the air, the mist clears away. After cold nights tiny drops of water can form on cold blades of grass. This is called dew.

Early morning mist on a meadow

Fogging up the river

Air is full of water vapor. When warm air cools, the water vapor forms a cloud of water droplets. If this happens near the ground, fog or mist is formed. Fog often forms over cold oceans, rivers, and lakes, as it has on this river in Southeast Asia.

Fun in the snow

Snow forms high inside clouds when the temperature is low. It is made of tiny crystals of ice. Raindrops often start to fall as ice crystals, but melt on the way down to Earth. In cold weather ice crystals reach the ground as snowflakes. A heavy snowfall covers the ground like a thick, white blanket. Frost and ice also form when the weather is very cold.

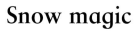

Snow magic

Snowflakes appear to be round and white. But each one is actually a beautiful ice crystal with six sides. Like people, no two ice crystals are exactly the same.

Icicles form on roofs.

Ice-skating rinks are made of water that is smoothed flat as it freezes.

Snowmen and snowballs are made of wet snow that packs easily.

Ice crystals

In warm weather the snow on the top of a mountain can melt and tumble down as an avalanche.

Powder snow on the slopes is perfect for skiing.

Packed snow is smooth and slippery enough for sledding.

Frosty windows

When the weather is very cold, water vapor in the air freezes into different types of frost. Frost can form thick ice on the ground, or it can make patterns on glass (right).

The wildest weather

Eye in the center of the storm

Clockwise direction of cyclone wind

Typhoons, hurricanes, and cyclones spiral in a counterclockwise direction in the Northern Hemisphere and in a clockwise direction in the Southern Hemisphere.

When thunderstorms happen near the equator, they can be wild and dangerous. Sometimes storms build up over warm, tropical seas and join together to form hurricanes. These storms are also called typhoons or tropical cyclones. Hurricane winds reach speeds of up to 225 miles per hour. Some of these storms can be 500 miles wide and 9 miles high. They create huge waves out at sea that flood the land.

Twisters

Huge pillars of spiraling air sometimes form beneath thunderclouds. These are called tornadoes, or twisters. Low air pressure inside the tornado acts like a giant vacuum cleaner and sucks up the air around it—as well as anything that it passes over. The winds spinning inside a tornado can move at speeds of up to 250 miles per hour.

Tropical storms

Hurricanes, typhoons, and cyclones are violent storms. These storms are made up of a spiral of fast-moving wind around a calm center called the "eye." The storm brings heavy rain as well as strong winds. When hurricanes hit land, buildings are destroyed, trees are uprooted, and people can be injured.

Palm trees bend easily in the wind, so they do not usually break or become uprooted.

Spectacular skies

Although the weather may be hard to forecast, it doesn't usually surprise us. Bright, sunny days follow cloudy or rainy days. But the weather can create beautiful, and terrible, spectacles. Rainbows appear after rain, and in certain parts of the world, the night sky can light up with colored lights called auroras. During a violent thunderstorm, large lumps of ice, called hail, may crash down to Earth from the sky.

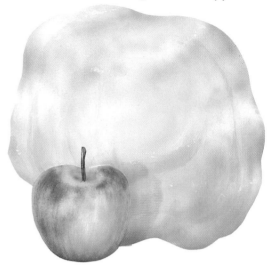

Some hailstones are larger than apples.

Raining ice

Hailstones are lumps of solid ice made inside a thundercloud. As they move around in the cloud, they collect water droplets, which freeze. The hailstones grow, usually up to half an inch around, and fall as hail.

Colors in the sky

In the arctic and antarctic regions, the Sun's rays sometimes react with gases in the thermosphere to create a colorful light show. Bands of red, green, and yellow lights fill the night sky. These are known as the aurora borealis (northern lights) in the Northern Hemisphere, and the aurora australis (southern lights) in the Southern Hemisphere.

Rainbows

A rainbow is caused by sunlight passing through millions of raindrops in the sky. As rays of light pass through the water droplets, they are broken up into seven colors—red, orange, yellow, green, blue, indigo, and violet. The colors are always the same and appear in the same order. You can only see a rainbow when the Sun is behind you.

Rainbow after a storm in Africa

Climate in crisis

Since the last ice age, the climate on Earth has been getting warmer. In recent years changes have happened more quickly. Because more coal and oil have been burned, the level of carbon dioxide in the atmosphere is increasing. This gas stops heat from escaping into space and makes the Earth warmer. This "greenhouse effect" is damaging our planet. We have to stop polluting the atmosphere if we want to save Earth!

Acid rain

Pollution from factories mixes with water in the air to create acid rain. This rain destroys plants, damages buildings, and kills fish in the rivers. Acid rain is carried by the wind and causes damage over a wide area.

Rising sea levels

Many scientists believe that air pollution is increasing the planet's temperature. Over the next 50 years Earth may get so much warmer that ice at the poles will melt, and the sea levels will rise and flood low-lying shores and islands.

Glossary

acid rain Rainwater that is full of pollution, which makes it acidic. Acid rain causes damage to trees, crops, and buildings.

air pressure The weight of air on the surface of Earth, measured with a barometer.

anemometer An instrument used for measuring wind speed.

atmosphere The air that surrounds Earth. It is made up of a mixture of gases, including nitrogen, oxygen, and water vapor.

climate The normal weather conditions that happen in a place over 30 years or more.

condensation The change of a gas into a liquid, such as water vapor into droplets of water.

desert An area of land where less than 10 in. of rain falls every year. Deserts can be either hot or cold.

drought Long periods of time when little or no rain falls.

equator An imaginary line around the center of Earth.

evaporation When a liquid changes into a gas—for example, when river water, heated by the Sun's rays, becomes water vapor.

fog Water droplets in the air that make it difficult to see.

fuels Substances, such as coal, wood, or gasoline, that we burn to make power. Among other things, this power can be used to heat our homes.

greenhouse effect Gases such as carbon dioxide build up in the atmosphere and stop heat on Earth from escaping into space. This raises Earth's temperature and causes the "greenhouse effect."

high pressure When the weight of the air on Earth is high.

humid The weather is humid when the air is moist or damp.

hurricane A violent, tropical storm that brings wind and rain. A hurricane can also be called a typhoon or a tropical cyclone.

lightning Electricity that has built up inside a cloud and then jumps to Earth in a bright flash.

low pressure When the weight of the air on Earth is low.

meteorite A chunk of rock that crashes to Earth from space. Most are small, but some are big and can cause huge explosions.

mist Water droplets floating in the air. Mist is similar to fog, but it lies closer to the ground.

monsoon A wind that blows off the sea onto the land for six months, and then blows the other way for six months.

Northern Hemisphere The half of Earth north of the equator.

poles Points at the top and bottom of Earth. The North Pole is in the arctic region, and the South Pole is in the antarctic region.

pollution Poisons in the environment that make us sick.

sea level The normal height of the surface of the sea.

season A period of weather lasting three to six months.

Southern Hemisphere The half of Earth south of the equator.

Sun The star at the center of our solar system, which Earth moves around, or orbits.

temperature The level of hotness of a body or substance.

thermometer An instrument that is used to measure temperature.

tornado A column of wind that spirals from the ground up to a thunder cloud. Also called a twister, or a waterspout at sea.

trade winds Winds that are always blowing over the oceans.

tropics The hot regions of the world around the equator.

water cycle When water moves from rivers to the air and back to the land as rain.

water vapor Water in the form of a gas floating in the air.

Index

A

acid rain 30, 31
airplanes 4, 6
air pressure 6, 13, 14, 26, 31
altocumulus clouds 18
altostratus clouds 19
anemometers 6, 31
atmosphere 4, 6, 30, 31
aurora lights 4, 28
avalanches 25

B

barographs 6
barometers 6, 31
Beaufort Scale 14

C

cirrocumulus clouds 19
cirrostratus clouds 19
cirrus clouds 18, 19
climate 10, 30, 31
clouds 16, 17, 18–19
Coriolis effect 15
cumulonimbus clouds 18, 19, 20
cumulus clouds 19
cyclones 12, 26–27

D

deserts 8, 10, 31
dinosaurs 8
drought 12, 13, 31
dry season 11

E

electricity 7, 20–21
equator 10, 12, 15, 26, 31
evaporation 13, 16–17, 31
exosphere 4
eye of the storm 26, 27

F

fall 11
floods 11, 12, 26, 30
fog 5, 17, 18, 22–23, 31
forecasting 6
frost 11, 24–25

G

gases 4, 5, 7, 16, 30

glacial periods
   (ice ages) 8
glaciers 9
greenhouse
   effect 30, 31

H

hailstones 20, 28
helium gas 6
humidity 11, 31
hurricanes 12, 26–27, 31

I

ice 11, 18, 19, 24, 28, 30
ice age 8, 30
ice caps 9
ice crystals 18, 19, 24
interglacials 8

L

lightning 19, 20–21, 31
lightning conductors 21

M

mammoths 9
mesosphere 4
meteorites 4, 8, 31
meteorologists 6, 9
meteorology 6
mist 11, 18, 19, 23, 31
monsoon 11, 31

N

nimbostratus clouds 18
North Pole 9, 10, 15
Northern Hemisphere 11,
   28, 31
northern lights
   (aurora borealis) 28

P

polar climate 10
poles 9, 10, 15, 30, 31
pollution 7, 22, 30, 31

R

rain 11, 16–17, 28, 30
rainbow 28, 29
raindrops 16, 29
rain forest 10
rainfall 7, 20

S

satellites 4, 6

sea 6
seasons 10, 11, 31
smog 22
snow 5, 11, 17, 18, 24–25
solar power 7
solar-powered car 7
South Pole 10, 15
Southern Hemisphere 11, 28, 31
southern lights (aurora australis) 28
space 4, 6
space shuttle 4
spring 11
storms 13, 20, 26–27
stratocumulus clouds 19
stratosphere 4
stratus clouds 19
summer 11
Sun 7, 10, 12–13, 28, 31
sunlight 7, 29

T

temperate zone 10
temperature 6, 11,
   12, 13, 30, 31
thermometers
   6, 31
thermosphere 4,
   28
thunder 19, 20,
   26, 28
thunderstorms 11, 20–21, 26, 28
tornadoes 19, 26, 31
trade winds 15, 31
tropics 12, 13, 31
troposphere 4, 18
   twisters 26
      typhoons 12, 26–27

V

volcanic dust 8
volcanoes 8

W

water 16–17, 23, 30
water cycle 16–17, 31
water vapor 5, 13, 16, 23, 25, 31
weather balloons 4, 6
weather maps 6
weather stations 6
weather vanes 6
wet season 11
wind 7, 12, 13, 14–15, 26–27
wind turbines 7
winter 11